The Secret of a Happy Day

The Secret of a Happy Day

Meditations on Psalm 23

J. Wilbur Chapman

BAKER BOOK HOUSE
Grand Rapids, Michigan

Reprinted from the 1899 edition
published by the United Society of Christian Endeavor
Paperback edition issued 1979 by
Baker Book House Company
ISBN: 0-8010-2435-8

Foreword by William J. Petersen
copyrighted 1979 by
Baker Book House Company

Printed in the United States of America

FOREWORD

"Have a happy day" is a commonplace greeting today. In fact, it has almost replaced "Good morning, how are you?" in our daily parlance. But how? In this day of international uncertainty, national unrest, and personal insecurity, how can you be sure of having a happy day? What's the secret?

The author of this book, although virtually forgotten today, was a household name in Christian circles at the turn of the century. Some say that when Evangelist D. L. Moody was finishing his evangelistic ministry, he "laid his mantle" on J. Wilbur Chapman. At any rate, Chapman was the prince of American evangelists from about 1898 to his death in 1918.

Born in Indiana in 1859, Chapman became a Christian nineteen years later when he was attending college near Chicago. He went to one of Moody's revival meetings and afterwards the famed evangelist personally explained to him God's plan of salvation.

For ten years Chapman served as a Presbyterian minister before launching into evangelism and other endeavors in the 1890s. One of his first evangelistic assistants was Billy Sunday, the converted baseball player. Among his "other endeavors" during the 1890s was to help found the Winona Lake Bible Conference in Indiana and to serve as vice-president of Moody Bible Institute in Chicago. But Chapman's most illustrious ministry was still ahead of him. Working within the Presbyterian Church, he was made secretary of the denomination's committee on evangelism. (Later he was elected to the top post in the denomination, a rare honor for an evangelist.)

In 1905, he developed what he called the Chapman Simultaneous Evangelism Campaign. Today we might call it Saturation Evangelism or Evangelism-in-Depth. A good example of how it worked was in Philadelphia in 1908. Chapman divided the city into forty-two districts and brought in twenty-one assistant evangelists and twenty-one song-leaders to conduct meetings. For three weeks they held meetings in one-half of the city, and then for the next three weeks, they shifted simultane-

Foreword

ously to the other half. Over four hundred churches participated, and the total attendance and total response was far greater than that of Moody's revival campaign there three decades earlier.

It is said that Chapman brought "spiritual dignity and grace" to revivalism, because he rarely employed fiery pulpit techniques. He had the ability to work with churches of various denominations without compromising his own convictions. He also travelled extensively overseas in evangelistic campaigns in Asia, Australia, and Europe.

A short, rather shy man who wore "a pair of pince-nez perched on his pinched little nose," Chapman was not the type of man whom you would expect to see as the dominant evangelist of those pre-World War I years. But if you heard him preach, you would have no doubt about his ministry. It is said that his sermons always conveyed a "great tenderness of sympathy."

As you read this practical little book, I think you will feel the same "tenderness of sympathy" that characterized the spoken messages of this great evangelist, J. Wilbur Chapman.

WILLIAM J. PETERSEN

CONTENTS

———

INTRODUCTION

THREE thousand years have passed away since David sung this sweet song, and yet it is as new and fresh as if it had come to us this morning.

No passage of Scripture has been more variously named or quoted.

One has called it his creed, learned at his mother's knee, repeated every day of his life, and to be lived by until the good Shepherd was seen face to face.

Another has named it the minstrel song, and as such it has sung hope into the hopeless, strength to the weak, courage into the army of the disappointed ; and it shall continue its ministry until the last one of God's children is called home. Then it will wing its way back to God from whom it came.

Henry Ward Beecher said it was "the nightingale song," for it sung its sweetest music in the night-time of disappointment and distress.

In my own thought of it, it has always been the song of the *meadow-lark*, for it is the habit of this bird to sing only as it leaves the earth, and the higher it flies, the sweeter it sings.

So this sweet song of David's is appreciated only by those who are "in the world and not of it," and who, according to Paul's injunction, live in the heavenlies. The Christian in touch with the world appreciates it not. One of my friends told me of his standing beside the open grave of his mother, when suddenly one of these meadow-larks started up from the dry grass by his side ; and, as it rose, it began its song, rising in its flight until it could not be seen, but its music fell like a benediction upon the sorrowing hearts. Upon every child of God standing beside the grave of buried hopes and lost joys this psalm breathes its blessing.

Its position is not to be forgotten, for the place where God has set it makes it a comfort to us all. It follows the twenty-second psalm, not because of the order of the numerals, and precedes the twenty-fourth, not for the same reason, but because the twenty-second is the psalm of the cross, and that is past, while the twenty-fourth is the psalm of the glory, and this is future. Thus these two psalms rise before us like two mountain peaks, leaving the twenty-third a fruitful, restful, refreshing valley between, with truth, not for the end of life alone, but for every step of the journey from the point of regeneration to the moment of translation to the skies.

"As a brook among the hills, making music through the year, and refreshing weary and thirsty wayfarers, so these words have spoken to the heart of many : of the peace of the fold, of the limpid lake, of the green glen, of the cool of overhanging rocks, of the comfort of protectorship, of the home where the spread table and the anointed head bespeak the day's work done, and mirror the complete rest and satisfaction of the soul. Then, taking every similitude, the Psalmist flings the necklace of pearls at the feet of Christ, declaring that this would be the condition of soul for all who knew his voice, and followed him as their shepherd.''

Every tense may be rendered by the present. "I do not want ; he leads me ; he makes me lie down ; he refreshes ; he guides ; I fear no evil ; they follow me." Not in the days that are to be, but to-day. Not in some scene which is yet to unfold or in some distant future, but here and now, if only thou wilt take him from this moment to be thy Shepherd, and wilt commence to obey his lead, and trust his watchful care.

For me to say anything new about this twenty-third psalm is indeed a difficult task, but to say anything at all that would be helpful is to put a writer's readers in his debt. In a little clipping which came one day to my table my eye lighted on an arrangement of the truth of this song of the meadow-lark which has never left me. It is well known that when once one has caught a vision of the constellations in the heavens, he cannot possibly in after nights be blind to them. In this same way I have never read the twenty-third psalm since that day when it has not fallen into six divisions, each with a name and each name beginning with the same letter.

This is the order, and for its helpfulness to me I owe
my unknown friend a debt of gratitude.

POSSESSION : The Lord is *my* shepherd, verse 1.
POSITION :   He maketh me *to lie down* in green
                      pastures.
                      He leadeth me *beside still waters*, verse 2.
PROMISE :   He *restoreth my soul*, verse 3.
PROGRESS :   *Yea, though I walk through* the valley,
                      verse 4.
PROVISION :   *Thou preparest a table before me*, verse 5.
PROSPECT :   *Goodness and mercy shall follow me*,
                      verse 6.

This is in a very peculiar way the song for the quiet
hour. One could not live in its truth without having
sweet fellowship with Him of whom the psalm sings.

It has been said that every valley in the Scriptures has
in it a well or spring of water. Whether this be true
or not, we do know that, if this psalm be likened unto
a valley, then we may find here that water which springs
up into everlasting life, and which if a man keep drinking
he shall never thirst.

May God make this little book a blessing to the many
Comrades of the Quiet Hour. The messages were deliv-
ered at the Detroit Quiet Hour meetings, when the
divisions suggested above were followed ; but now for the
sake of my readers they are presented in the form of a
meditation for each day of the month.

May every reader in every day of thought meet Him with whom it is our privilege each moment to abide.

> "I have a Friend so precious,
>   So very dear to me,
> He loves me with such tender love,
>   He loves so faithfully,
> I could not live apart from him,
>   I love to feel him nigh;
> And so we dwell together,
>   My Lord and I."

J. WILBUR CHAPMAN

THE
SECRET OF A HAPPY DAY

———•———

First Day

" The LORD is my shepherd."

IT is said that whenever we find the Lord's name written in small capitals in the Old Testament, we are to remember that the thought is to be concerning Jehovah. The Israelites spoke his name but once a year, and then the high priest was the speaker, and the place was the most holy place. They had such a reverence, not only for Jehovah but also for his very name, that they would not set their feet upon a piece of parchment for fear his name might be upon the other side. And he whom Israel thus reverenced is your Lord for this day. Is there any reason why it may not be a day of victory?

In different places in the Old Testament this very name Jehovah is used with added emphasis, as if to make plain what he would be to Israel.

Jehovah; that is, "I am that I am," Exod. 6 : 3.   Since we live in the New Testament times, it is our privilege to finish the sentence, making him to be all that our souls long for.   I am thy life, thy strength, thy soul's delight; "I will guide thee with mine eye."

Jehovah-jireh, Gen. 22 : 14; that is, "The Lord will provide."   "No good thing will he withhold from them that walk uprightly."   Every hour of this day his strength shall counteract thy weakness; his rest shall be in place of thy restlessness; he himself shall guard thee from every ill.

Jehovah-nissi; that is, "Jehovah my banner," Exod. 17 : 15.   There was to be fighting that day with Amalek, and Moses knew that victory was his because Jehovah was his secret of strength. There will be temptations for you this day, but temptation is not sin; yielding is sin.   But no temptation can overtake you and cause defeat if the Lord be given the mastery of your life.

Jehovah-shalom; that is, "Jehovah send peace," Judg. 6 : 24.   And he will give peace in the place of unrest, because he gives himself.   It is every Christian's privilege to claim the Lord in all his fulness.   Do this for to-day, and victory is certain.

SUGGESTIONS FOR TO-DAY

1. Realize, if you can, your own weakness. This will show you how dangerous your position is and how liable you are to fall.

2. Conceive, if you can, his mighty strength, and then realize that he is yours to stand between you and every temptation and trial.

3. Over and over this day keep saying, "If God be for me, who can be against me?"

4. Commit your way to him, and let him be responsible at least for this one day of your life.

Second Day

"The Lord IS my shepnerd."

HE is our present helper. There is such a tendency to put him out of our lives. In truth he is with us all the time; in practical experience he is in the heavens, and we only wait for the day when we shall see him. But he is yours to-day; "Lo, I am with you alway" is for you *now*.

Cultivate the habit of thinking of him as at your side. Speak to him as if he were your dearest friend. Walk with him; go only where he would go or you could take him. Take no step of which he could not approve. He will thus become your present help in every time of trouble and of need.

> "Sometimes I'm faint and weary;
> He knows that I am weak;
> And, as he bids me lean on him,
> His help I gladly seek;

He leads me in the paths of light,
Beneath a sunny sky;
And so we walk together,
My Lord and I."

We sometimes make the mistake of setting our stakes too far ahead, as marking out the time when we shall have fellowship with him; but for to-morrow and its needs we need not pray, but "just for to-day."

Let this day mark a new experience. Begin the day by appropriating him, with all that that means; for *he is yours*. Then set the mark on until ten o'clock, and say, "For those two hours I will walk in the thought that he is mine." Then lengthen the time until the noon hour; and whatsoever you do, whether you eat or drink or whatsoever you do, do all to the glory of God. If half the day may be thus lived, the whole day may be.

In all this time make every act of yours true worship. As you cleanse your hands, let it draw you to him whose blood may keep you unspotted from the world; as you put on your garments, let it remind you of him whom you have been commanded "to put on"; as you drink, forget not him who said, "I am the water of life"; and, as you eat, call to your remembrance your Lord who said, " I am the bread of life; he that cometh to me shall never hunger." Dr. Floyd Tompkins says, " Thus every act of every day may be like a sacrament." And a day thus lived, if repeated for a week, may become the habit of your life, and all because the Lord IS yours.

SUGGESTIONS FOR TO-DAY

1. Do not live in the past to-day; for, if you were a sinner above all others, then God for Christ's sake " hath put away thy sin," and for-given sin with God is remembered no more forever.

2. Do not live in the future. He will care for you to-morrow, and you may never see it. Why take thought for it?

3. Live in the present. He is yours to-day, and for all the hours of this day you will have what all the saints in all the ages have had to make them great and good.

Third Day

"The Lord is MY shepherd."

MARTIN LUTHER once said that most of experimental religion would be found in the personal and possessive pronouns of the Bible, and that is certainly true of this psalm, for here we find only six verses, and they contain only one hundred and eighteen words, and in this brief list twenty-eight pronouns may be counted. He called this psalm a little Bible, and well he might; for, if we had only this, we should certainly come to know the Lord, and when we know him we always trust him.

In the brevity of it it is like a short ladder, but it is long enough to reach from the gloom of this present evil day up to the brightness and glory of the perfect day; it is really, if properly understood, a ladder of three rounds; namely, out of self, into Christ, and into glory. But there is really no part of the psalm that brings more comfort than your appropriation of him in the use of this pronoun "my."

It will bring rejoicing where otherwise there would be despair; it will inspire a song where there might have been a groan; it will put a silver lining on every cloud; it will gird you with strength for every temptation. Say it over and over to-day, "He is *my* shepherd; he is MY shepherd." This little word will make a paradise of earth, and fill with glory the home where you live and the place where you work; in a word, it will lift you up to the heavenlies. The water-spider forms a sac-like cottage, and fills it with air; then shuts herself in and sinks into the sea. She then anchors it and there brings forth her young, she practically lives in an upper world, although surrounded by all the dangers of the great deep. This is your privilege for this day and every day to live in the very atmosphere of heaven while working down here in the sin-tainted atmosphere of this world.

It is this personal appropriation of Christ that makes this world like heaven. It is this sweet fellowship that opens our eyes, so that again and again we cannot help saying, " Thou knowest that I love thee."

" He knows how much I love him,
   He knows I love him well,
But with what love he loveth me
   My tongue can never tell ;
It is an everlasting love,
   An ever rich supply ;
And so we love each other,
   My Lord and I."

SUGGESTIONS FOR TO-DAY

1. Put aside generalities to-day. It is wonderful to say, The Lord is *a* shepherd, but it is better far to say, He is MINE. Let this day be lived in the preciousness of it.

2. If he is yours, then he will be to you what every shepherd in the New Testament is pictured as being to the sheep. He will seek you when wandering, find you when lost, hold you when found, and shield you from every harm.

3. There is no excuse for failure to-day with such a shepherd, and him all yours.

Fourth Day

"The Lord is MY shepherd."

THIS psalm belongs to us if we can truthfully say these first five words; then the rest of the psalm is our spiritual possession.

One of my friends was telling me the story of a traveller in Switzerland. He was a Christian. One day he came across a little shepherd boy to whom he told the story of the good Shepherd who had given his life for the sheep. He tried to teach him the twenty-third psalm; but the little fellow could not read, and so made slow work of it. At last the man said to him, " I will tell you how to read a part of it on your fingers. Just take the first five words, and you will have a word for each finger." So the little fellow counted the words on his fingers, " The Lord is my Shepherd." This was only to keep them in his memory.

A while after that the same traveller was passing through Switzerland again, and thought he would look up his little shepherd boy. He came to the place where he had lived, and was met by the mother of the lad, who in answer to the inquiry concerning her boy said that he was dead. The gentleman expressed his sorrow, and said that he had hoped to see him again.

Then the mother said, " Are you the man that taught my boy to say something on his fingers ? " He replied that he was. Then she said to him, " My boy, just before he died, told me to tell you, if you ever came this way again, that he died holding the fourth finger of his hand." The little fellow was just laying claim to the possessive pronoun " my."

I think I should like to die like that. But it is better far to know that we may live claiming this promise. He is *my* shepherd — all that he is is mine, his mind, his peace, his meekness, his gentleness, indeed, his spirit, all my own.

There is surely thus no excuse for failure, and there can be no reason why we should go astray.

> " Thou art my light and my salvation ;
>   Of whom shall I be afraid ? "

SUGGESTIONS FOR TO-DAY

1. Try to realize that everything in the good Shepherd is yours for to-day just as truly as if

there were no one else to be considered but yourself.

2. By an act of appropriating faith lay claim to everything in him that you lack in yourself, his patience for your impatience, his strength for your weakness. In every case claim from him the grace opposite to your failing.

3. Remember that no mistake of yours in the past affects his love for to-day. The record is all clean; you can make it what you will.

Fifth Day

"The Lord is my SHEPHERD."

DAVID knew how he loved his sheep, and so no more endearing name could be given to his Lord.

He is called "the chief Shepherd" by Peter in 1. Pet. 5 : 4; for Peter was looking for him to appear, and he knew him to be the chiefest among ten thousand. And Peter's longing may be fulfilled to-day. So live this day in the light, the hope, and the power of his appearing.

In John he is called "the good Shepherd." John 10 : 11. "I am the good shepherd; the good shepherd giveth his life for the sheep." Then in the same chapter is given a description of what would really seem to be the sheepfold, when it is written, "They shall never perish, neither shall any man pluck them out of my hand." John 10 : 28.

What a resting-place that is! What security is there!

But the next verse increases the sweetness and power of the thought. "My Father, which gave them me, is greater than all; and no man is able to pluck them out of my Father's hand." John 10 : 29. And it is as if the Father's hand had just been placed over us as we rest in the hand of Christ. This is indeed the sheepfold; and, if this is our place in the plan of God, then surely nothing can molest us or make us afraid.

But the next verse really increases the comfort of the thought, when Jesus says, "I and my Father are one." John 10 : 30. One in holding us out to the end. One in protecting us from danger and from harm. One in love toward us; for, having loved us, the love will be unto the end.

Granted the fact that yours is a life of discouragement, that everything in life seems to be against you. Every day may be a day of blessing, every hour an hour of victory, if but lived in the thought that Jehovah in his might is your shepherd, in sympathy, in love, and in helpfulness.

SUGGESTIONS FOR TO-DAY

1. It is the shepherd's business to lead his sheep to the place where they may find food

to eat and water to drink. Our Shepherd will do this for you to-day.

2. But you must be most sensitive to his leadings. It would be well to pause frequently to-day, and see whether he is really leading you on.

3. Do not dare go through the day without feeding upon his word. One verse may drive away the adversary of your soul. Stop often and take a deep breath of the very life of God.

Sixth Day

"The Lord is my SHEPHERD."

THERE are two things to be constantly borne in mind in connection with the shepherd's life, not only that he cares for the weak sheep, and goes seeking for wandering sheep, but —

1. The shepherd generally in his watch-care over the flock takes his position on some place of elevation. In this way he is able to protect the interests of his sheep, and our Shepherd is thus exalted, and at the right hand of God he has taken his seat. He is not standing, for that would indicate a work not completed, and after the order of men, but seated, as our high priest. Heb. 10 : 11, 12.

Do you remember how, when our Master took with him Peter and James and John and went into the garden of Gethsemane, he left the chosen three and went into the deepening shadows alone to pray? In the midst of his prayer he came back again to his disciples for a word of sympathy, and found them sleeping. Have you ever noticed the sentence recorded just at that point? It is this: "For their eyes were heavy." It is the explanation given by our Master, and recorded by the Holy Ghost, for their apparent failure. It was as if he had said, "Poor men, they are tired out; they have had no rest; their eyes were heavy; it is not because they are indifferent." And it is just this kind of explanation which he is making before God to-day, for you and for me, in the time of our weakness.

2. The shepherd always stands between his sheep and danger, and our Shepherd does the same. If we are living where we ought to live, and in right relations with him, he will turn aside the darts of the evil one; but, if our walk is out of fellowship, and our hearts are not right, it will be perfectly natural and easy for us to fall.

So to-day, when temptation comes, put Christ between you and it. When sin finds lodgment in your heart, break with it instantly in his power, for the least sin, encouraged and not forsaken, will lead you to awful defeat and despair. No child of God is strong enough to resist evil if he is out of fellowship with Christ. Put him between you and every thought of sin.

SUGGESTIONS FOR TO-DAY.

1. Confess sin *instantly* to-day. Bear in mind that he is at the right hand of God to intercede for you.

2. Bear in mind that men who have made ship-wreck of their lives began with a sin as small as the sin in your life of yesterday.

3. For to-day guard the point where you failed yesterday, not by the power of resolution, but by placing him between you and that danger. He is ever the secret of victory over sin.

Seventh Day

" I shall not WANT."

You will notice David does not say, " I shall not *need*; " it is by far a better word he uses, " I shall not *want*." We often want many things we do not need; but, the more we come to understand that the Lord is our Shepherd, the more our wants and needs become identical, and we can say, as David said, " I shall not *want*." If this twenty-third psalm be the valley of our present-day experience, then we shall want for nothing he does not supply.

" I shall not want rest. ' He maketh me to lie down in green pastures.'

" I shall not want drink. ' He leadeth me beside the still waters.'

" I shall not want forgiveness. ' He restoreth my soul.'

" I shall not want guidance. ' He guideth me in the paths of righteousness for his name's sake.'

" I shall not want companionship. ' Yea, though

I walk through the valley of the shadow of death, I will fear no evil; for thou art with me.'

"I shall not want comfort. 'Thy rod and thy staff they comfort me.'

"I shall not want food. 'Thou preparest a table before me in the presence of mine enemies.'

"I shall not want joy. 'Thou hast anointed my head with oil.'

"I shall not want anything. 'My cup runneth over.'

"I shall not want anything in this life. 'Surely goodness and mercy shall follow me all the days of my life.'

"I shall not want anything in eternity. For 'I will dwell in the house of the Lord forever.'

"That is what David said he would find in the good Shepherd. And one day it occurred to me to see how this twenty-third psalm was fulfilled in Christ. This is what I found in Christ's own words : —

"'I am the good Shepherd.'

"Thou shalt not want rest. 'Come unto me all ye that labor and are heavy laden, and I will give you rest.'

"Thou shalt not want drink. 'If any man thirst, let him come unto me and drink.'

"Thou shalt not want forgiveness. 'The Son of man hath power on earth to forgive sins.'

"Thou shalt not want guidance. 'I am the way, and the truth, and the life.'

"Thou shalt not want companionship. 'Lo, I am with you all the days.'

"Thou shalt not want comfort. 'The Father shall give you another Comforter.'

"Thou shalt not want food. 'I am the bread of life; he that cometh to me shall not hunger.'

"Thou shalt not want joy. 'That my joy may be in you, and that your joy may be filled full.'

"Thou shalt not want anything. 'If ye shall ask anything of the Father in my name, he will give it to you.'

"Thou shalt not want anything in this life. 'Seek ye first his kingdom and his righteousness, and all these things shall be added unto you.'

"Thou shalt not want anything in eternity. 'I go to prepare a place for you, that where I am there ye may be also.'" — *Mrs. John R. Mott.*

SUGGESTIONS FOR TO-DAY

1. When you pray this morning, plead God's promise. Be very definite about it. He had you in mind when he made it.

2. As you walk to-day, go in the consciousness that " no good thing will he withhold from them that walk uprightly."

3. If for a brief moment you fear that you are out of fellowship with him, get alone with him. Plead his promise for his own presence, peace, and power; and he will keep his word.

You shall not want.

Eighth Day

"He maketh me to lie down in green
pastures."

"THE Christian life has two elements in it, the
contemplative and the active; and both of these
are richly provided for." The text above intro-
duces us to the *contemplative*.

"In a hilly country like Palestine, under a burn-
ing sun, only the glens or valleys were covered
with the green herbage, which was refreshing and
satisfying to the flock. If I should write that the
Lord hath green pastures for us, I could present
the thought of the riches of his provision for us;
but, when I say he will lead us into this place of
refreshment, I present to you the thought of his
goodness and his grace."

"But the slopes of Palestine, bared to the hot
sun of the East, are not more parched and barren
than the portion of the world through which you
will be obliged to walk this day; so without
the green pastures it will be a sad experience

What are these green pastures but the Scriptures of truth, always fresh, always rich, and never exhausted ? "

As with a new-born babe food is the requisite, proper nourishment it must have, so the fresh pasture of the word of God is opened, the knowledge of his will revealed, the delight of his fulness unfolded, and perfect satisfaction is offered. " When by faith we are enabled to find rest in the promises, we are like the sheep that lie down, and we find both provender and peace, rest and refreshment."

It is said that hungry sheep never lie down. Why is it, then, that so many of God's children seem famished and are not comfortable in him ? It is because they are taken up with the world, because they are feeding upon husks, because they have turned their faces away from the truth, but more truly still because they have refused to hear his voice leading them into all this restfulness and satisfaction. It is God's will that we should be filled with peace.

SUGGESTIONS FOR TO-DAY

Begin the day in quietness. Get alone, if only for a little while, with God. Give him the right of way in your life; breathe in of his gracious presence; keep very still before him, and let this be in the early part of the day.

Why in the Morning?

At a meeting of Morning Bible-Readers held lately in Calcutta the following reasons were given why we should read the Bible and pray in the morning.

1. We owe first things to God.

2. We are most likely to be able to secure a quiet time in the morning.

3. There is much danger that Bible-study and prayer will be crowded out entirely if not enjoyed in the morning.

4. The mind is then free and fresh.

5. First impressions last.

6. Bible-study and prayer make a good foundation for the day.

7. We should seek a high-level start.

8. By this we are put on guard against sin. Ps. 119 : 9, 11.

9. We shall most probably have occasion during the day to use what we get in the morning. One should not go out into wild districts without weapons and ammunition.

10. Many good and holy persons recommend this as one of the chief secrets of deep spiritual living.

11. There is biblical authority for the habit. See Ps. 5 : 3, and elsewhere.

Ninth Day

"He leadeth me."

"THE other side of the Christian experience is to be found in gracious activity. We not only think, but we act. We are not always lying down to feed or because we are satisfied, but we are journeying on toward perfection. But it must all be under his leadership. The shepherd leads the way; the flock, confiding from experience in his wisdom and goodness, follow. 'And when he putteth forth his own sheep, he goeth before them, and the sheep follow him : for they know his voice.' John 10 : 4. In ordinary circumstances the shepherd does not feed his flock; he simply guides them where they may gather for themselves; but there are times when it is otherwise. Take in the autumn, when the pastures are dried up, and in winter in places covered with snow, he must furnish them food or they die; and so it is not an uncommon sight to see the shepherd all day long in the bushy trees, cutting down the branches upon whose green leaves and tender twigs the sheep are entirely supported.   Mary was the sister sitting at her Master's feet in contemplation, Martha the sister busy serving, constantly in action; but, as they both dwelt in one house, so must both these elements of the Christian life be in one heart."

"It is a mistake to think the life may be right without the green-pasture experience, and quite as much of a mistake to think that there can be genuine satisfaction without service.   So our good Shepherd will feed us as he leads us out to live for him."

There must be the reflection of his life in all we do.   There must be the inflection of his voice in all we say.   There must be the heavenly atmosphere of his presence in all that we are.   Our Christian life is a failure if it is not possible for all with whom we come in contact to take "knowledge of us that we have been with Jesus."

> "He knows how I am longing
>   Some weary soul to win,
> And so he bids me go and speak
>   The loving word to him;
> He bids me tell his wondrous love,
>   And why he came to die;

And so we work together,
  My Lord and I."

SUGGESTIONS FOR TO-DAY

1. Begin the day by enthroning him in your life. Make him your king as never before, and yield to him your loyal submission.

2. Make a covenant with him that there shall be only one path for you this day, and that the way in which he will walk before you.

3. Make a firm resolve that the day shall make some person happier, his burden lighter, his trouble easier to bear, because you touched them with your influence.

4. Make grateful acknowledgment to the Lord for the privilege of walking with him one entire day.

Tenth Day

" Beside the still waters."

It is at least suggestive that in the contemplation of the whole of this second verse of this psalm we have in outline the possible experience of every child of God for every day; first the green pastures, then his undisputed leadership, then the still waters. Every day must begin with feeding, go on in active service, and end with quiet contemplation of his mercy and his goodness. So, because it is often more difficult to use a victory than to gain one, this suggestion is made for the day.

It is said that sheep will never drink of the turbulent stream, but only at the still waters. How true it is that there must be still hours in our lives if we would grow and be girded with strength! The day which began with feeding must end in quiet thoughtfulness if we would keep in fellowship with the Lord, and absorb his beauty of holiness.

What are these " still waters " but the influence and graces of the Spirit of God?   His Spirit attends us in various ways like " waters " — in the plural number, you will notice   to cleanse, to refresh, and to strengthen.   But he cannot be appreciated or appropriated in his transforming power until we have learned the lesson of waiting before him in perfect quietness.   I have found six positions for the child of God, —

In his hand for safety. — John 10 : 28.

At his feet to be taught. — Luke 8 : 35.

On his shoulder for support. — Luke 15 : 5.

At his side for fellowship. — John 21 : 20.

In his arms for rest. — Deut. 33 : 27.

Beside the still waters for refreshment. — Ps. 23 : 2.

" That silence is golden indeed in which the Holy Spirit meets with the souls of his saints. Not to raging waves of strife, but to peaceful streams of holy love, does the Spirit of God conduct the chosen sheep.   He is a dove, not an eagle; the dew, not the hurricane.   And our Lord leads us to these still waters; we could not go of ourselves."

SUGGESTIONS FOR TO-DAY

1. Yield absolutely for this whole day to his leadership; make no reservation.

2. Commit to memory Ps. 119:11, "Thy word have I hid in mine heart, that I might not sin against thee." 1 Cor. 10:13.

3. When tempted, claim the victory, because of the Lord's promise. When irritable, claim his peace and rest.

4. When the day is over, confess to him your mistakes, thank him for your triumph over weakness and sin.

5. Before you close your eyes in sleep talk to him as to an earthly friend; tell him your joys, your sorrows, your disappointments, and the failures you have made.

> " I tell him all my sorrows,
>   I tell him all my joys,
> I tell him all that pleases me,
>   I tell him what annoys;
> He tells me what I ought to do,
>   He tells me what to try;
> And so we talk together,
>   My Lord and I. "

Eleventh Day

" He restoreth my soul."

" WHEN the soul grows sorrowful, he revives it;
when it is sinful, he sanctifies it; when it is weak,
he strengthens it. *He* does it. His ministers
could not do it if he did not; his word would not
avail by itself."

The believer is liable to fall; but to fall and to
fall away are two quite different experiences. Peter
fell, until he struck the prayers of Him who said,
" Satan hath desired *you*, but I have prayed for
thee." The fifteenth of Luke is the *lost* chapter
for the Christian; and it is possible for us, like
the coin, to be lost and still be in the house; for
our place to be as an adornment for our risen
Head, as the lost piece of silver, and yet be on the
floor and for that reason useless; but, as the sheep
had its shepherd, the money its owner, the prodigal his father, so we have our Lord to whom we
may offer the prayer, " Restore my soul, O thou
shepherd of the sheep."

The same hand which first rescued us from

46

ruin reclaims us from wandering; and, when he restores, it is to the same standing that we had before our fall from fellowship. Some one has said that that expression of the prodigal's father, "Bring forth the best robe," is literally, "Bring forth the same old robe he used to wear," which teaches that, when the prodigal went home, it was to have the same standing he had before his awful blunder.

We must have restoration, for of what use would be the green pastures and a soul out of tune with God?

We must have placed upon us his hand, and hear his voice saying, "Peace, be still"; for of what use would be the still waters if our souls were turbulent and distressed?

You may be lost to the holiness, the happiness, the peace, the power, that once was yours. If so, you need his restoring touch. If you were ever higher spiritually than you are to-day, you have fallen just the difference between that higher point and this.

SUGGESTIONS FOR TO-DAY

1. Find out what it is that has robbed you of your peace and joy. The responsibility cannot be upon God; it must be with you.

2. Confess your faults to God or to men as you may have sinned against them. Remember you are no more nearly right with God than with your fellow men.

3. Believe that what you have honestly confessed he will freely forgive.

4. Breathe in once again of his fulness.

5. Ask him for special help for the day, which may be yours on the morrow; then rest in him.

Twelfth Day

"He restoreth my soul."

THERE are certain tests by means of which we may know whether we are in need of restoring grace.

Sometimes, alas! we so hurry along in the race of life that we do not realize how far we have drifted from God. The literal rendering of Heb. 2 : 1 may be, "Therefore we ought to give the more earnest heed to the things which we have heard, lest at any time we should drift away from them." Heedlessness often causes drifting. These may be tests, according to Mr. Meyer : —

1. *Restlessness*, a general dissatisfaction with ourselves and everything about us. Nothing seems right; everybody is wrong; we are content with no one thing beyond a passing moment. This is a sure indication of a drifting away from Him who said, "Take my yoke upon you . . . and ye shall find rest unto your souls."

"I have his yoke upon me,
     And easy 't is to bear;
In the burden which he carries
     I gladly take a share;
For then it is my happiness
     To have him always nigh, —
To bear the yoke together,
     My Lord and I."

2. A lack of interest in the things of the Kingdom. How can two walk together except they be agreed? Since all the power of heaven contributes to the advancement of the kingdom of God, it is clear proof that your life is contrary to the plan of God if your interest is waning.

3. A spirit of impatience and intolerance with others is one of the surest indications that there is a letting down in spiritual force and fervor. "If a man be overtaken in a fault, ye which are spiritual restore such a one in the spirit of meekness." So, if it is your disposition to criticise and not to restore, you are in need of restoring grace yourself. We ought to have the forgiving spirit, the spirit of charity, the spirit of helpfulness toward the weaker member of the body of Christ. Any other disposition than this is not his mind; but, if we have failed, we need not be discouraged.

"Have you missed in your aim? Well, the mark is
   still shining;
Did you faint in the race? Well, take breath for the
   next;
Did the clouds drive you back? But see yonder their
   lining;
Were you tempted and fell? Let it serve for a text."

SUGGESTIONS FOR TO-DAY

1. Claim the opposite grace from Christ; that
is, if impatient, claim his patience; if weak, his
strength; if restless, his peace; if defeated, take
him as your victory over every enemy.

2. In your relations to the church and every
interest flowing out from it live for one day as
you think He would live whose name you bear.

3. In all your dealings with men until this day
is passed govern your actions by the question,
"What would Jesus do?"

Thirteenth Day

"He RESTORETH my soul."

THERE are certain causes for spiritual declension, and they are always to be found in ourselves.

It is true we have the old nature with us, while at the same time we have the *new* nature, the life of God, but it is no license for us to sin, for Paul writes, "The law of the spirit of life in Christ Jesus hath made me free from the law of sin and death." If you lived yesterday in the flesh, it was at the cost of the spirit. If you live to-day in the spirit, it shall be at the cost of the flesh.

There is really no excuse for failure if we are living as we ought to live, with Christ between us and temptation, and Christ between us and sin. But, because we have failed, it is well to know the reason; and it may be because —

1. There was some neglect of the Bible — it is

the bread of life, the water of life, the staff of life; and he will be a weak, trembling, falling Christian who lets one day pass without a little portion of it running through his life — like the light to reveal imperfections and like the water to make the temple clean.

2. It may be that there is some unconfessed sin hiding away in the secret recesses of your heart. The children of God do not leap into grievous sin at a bound; there was first some little sin that tarried, was courted, then encouraged to stay, and finally conceived and brought forth a brood of iniquity, which was strong enough to overthrow the ripest saint.

3. It may be that, when God called you to some service, you disobeyed; and disobedience puts you out of tune with heaven. The fact that you are in the world proves that you are indispensable to the working out of God's plan; the fact that he called you to do something for him clearly indicates that his will must be yours, or there is confusion and strife.

But, whatever the cause, he waits to restore you to the old strength, the lost peace, the old, sweet song that was formerly yours; and he will do it to-day.

SUGGESTIONS FOR TO-DAY

1. Start the day with the word of God, and remember that when Jesus won the victory over Satan he said, " It is written."

2. Confess your sins that are past ; and, if you fail to-day, confess to him *instantly*.

3. Whatsoever he saith unto you, *do it*.

4. Make a covenant, just for this day.

> " Lord, for to-morrow and its needs
>   I do not pray ;
> Keep me from stain of sin
>   Just for to-day ;
> Let me both diligently work
>   And duly pray,
> Let me be kind in deed and word,
>   Just for to-day ;
> Let me be slow to do my will,
>   Prompt to obey ;
> Help me to sacrifice myself,
>   Just for to-day.
>
> Let me no wrong nor idle word
>   Unthinking say,
> Set thou thy seal upon my lips,
>   Just for to-day.
> So for the morrow and its needs
>   I do not pray ;
> But keep me, guide me, hold me, Lord,
>   Just for to-day."

Fourteenth Day

"He leadeth me."

"THE Christian delights to be obedient, but it is the obedience of love to which he is constrained by the example of his Master."

If he is leading us, two or three things are true.

1. He will go before us, and he will select no way in which his sheep could not travel.

> "So on I go, not knowing;
> I would not if I might;
> I'd rather walk in the dark with God
> Than go alone in the light.
> I'd rather walk by faith with him
> Than go alone by sight."

If it be the path of sorrow, it is turned into rejoicing because he is with us; if it be the way of disappointment, change the *d* to an *h* and it will become "his appointment," and it will be our joy.

2. We must be like his bond-slaves as we go on; it is not, however, the slavery in which shackles keep us from freedom, but the spirit of that text, "Where the Spirit of the Lord is, there is liberty." It does not mean liberty for us to do as we please, for that is lawlessness; but rather liberty for him to do as he pleases with us; and that is all joy.

It is possible under certain conditions for the marble to be moulded like clay in the hands of the potter, and thus to become the statue of an angel; but this is nothing compared with the transformation which may be wrought in our lives, did he but have the right of way in them.

3. There can be only one way through this world for the child of God if this text be true, and that is the way where he can travel before us. In our attitude toward the world and our walk through it we must go only as he leads.

SUGGESTIONS FOR TO-DAY

1. Make a firm resolve that this day of your life shall be for his glory, and so let him lead you where he wills.

2. Remember his words, that "inasmuch as ye did it unto the least of these, you did it unto me."

Lift some one's burden to-day; cheer some one's downcast soul. This will please him.

3. If there is some one against whom you have a grudge, do that one a favor to-day. The chances are, your feelings will change entirely before the week is ended. Live and act to-day as you think Jesus would. This is allowing him to lead you.

Fifteenth Day

" He leadeth me."

THERE are certain ways by means of which we may surely detect the Lord's leadings.

His own example is an illustration. What did he do in circumstances so nearly like our own?

His instructions given his disciples in the Gospels may serve as guide-posts for us, pointing out the way in which we should walk. The advice of a friend may be the very clearest teaching of God.

The preaching of a sermon or the singing of a hymn may open clearly the way.

Those inner promptings of the Spirit which come we know not how are as a rule the leadings of God.

And, if two of these agree, it is at least well to consider carefully whether this may not be God's call to walk in the way of his own choosing. However, Henry Drummond has said in his

"Ideal Life," "Let it be remembered that it requires a well-kept life to will to do the will of God. It requires a well-kept life to *do* the will of God, and even a *better*-kept life to *will* to do his will. To be willing is a rarer grace than to be doing the will of God. For he who is *willing* may sometimes have nothing to *do*, and must only be willing to wait, and it is easier far to be doing God's will than to be willing to have nothing to do; it is easier far to be working for Christ than it is to be willing to cease. So there is nothing rarer in the world to-day than the truly willing soul, and there is nothing more worth coveting than the will to will God's will. There is no grander possession for any Christian life than the transparently simple mechanism of a sincerely obeying heart; and, if we could keep the machinery clear, there would be lives in thousands doing God's will on earth even as it is done in heaven."

> "Father, I know that all my life
>   Is portioned out for me;
> The changes that will surely come
>   I do not fear to see:
> I ask thee for a present mind,
>   Intent on pleasing thee."

SUGGESTIONS FOR TO-DAY

1. Tell him that for to-day at least you are perfectly willing to be led.

2. Wait patiently before you move, that you may know whether he is really going in advance of you. Remember that much of the chafing and disappointment and fret of life have come because you were impatient and moved before the pillar of cloud led you.

3. Do not say, "I cannot know his will; I am stupid about it all." This matters little to Christ, even if it be true. If he cannot make you understand in one way, he will in another. It is the business of the Shepherd to lead the willing sheep aright.

Sixteenth Day

" In the PATHS of righteousness."

" In another verse we were told that the Shepherd led beside still waters, and the inference might have been that, when the feet were cut, or the muscles strained by the clamber up the rocky mountain track, or that, when the course lay amid deep, damp glens, overshadowed by heavy forests and overhanging rocks, that at such times the sheep was following his own wild way, outside the tender guidance of its Lord. And so the Psalmist takes up the metaphor again, and tells us that there are other walks by which the Shepherd is leading us to our home. Not always beside the gentle streamlet flow, but sometimes by the foaming torrent; not always over the delicate grass, but sometimes up the stony mountain track; not always in the sunshine, but sometimes through the valley of the shadow of death. But whichever way it is, it is the right way and it is the way home."

John McNeill says it is literally, "He leadeth me in the sheep-tracks." If this be so, he leads in many different ways, from many different directions, but always in every way to the fold.

But the word "paths," says Rev. Ford C. Ottman, has another meaning in the Hebrew: it is literally wagon ruts. David had a fine reason for the use of this term. In the Holy Land the roads were not good, and the wagon wheels were constructed so as to meet this difficulty. These wheels were perhaps eighteen to twenty inches in width; and, as wheel after wheel would pass over the ground, it would wear a smooth path, and many a time David leading his sheep home would take to the wagon ruts because it was the easiest path for himself and his sheep. But all this is as nothing when compared with the way in which the Lord will lead us if we but yield absolutely to his leadership.

"Jesus, day by day
Near us in life's way,
Naught of dangers will we reckon,
Simply haste where thou dost beckon.

Lead us by the hand
To our Fatherland.
Thus our path shall be
Daily traced by thee.
Draw thou nearer when 't is rougher;
Help us most when most we suffer;
And, when all is o'er,
Ope to us thy door."

SUGGESTIONS FOR TO-DAY

1. You can bear the trials of the day because the way, though thorny, leads home.

2. You can endure the hardships of the passing hour, for strong souls always graduate from suffering into glory.

3. You can meet your temptations, fierce though they be, for God has with the temptation provided the way of escape.

4. This way is our good Shepherd, who goes before in every way of darkness and of trial, and leads us home.

Seventeenth Day

"In the paths of righteousness."

AND what can this mean but right paths?

In the wilderness of the desert there are no raised paths, the paths being merely tracks. They may run in different directions, and be most confusing. There must therefore be one who may choose the right paths for us. This our Shepherd is pledged to do. There have been times when you thought God's way was not best; there was nothing for you but mystery. But remember, "All things work together for good," not always happiness, nor peace, nor prosperity, in the judgment of men, but always for good.

In a cotton-mill every part of the work in all the factory works together for cotton cloth. In your life all is for good if you are where God would have you be.

"Only do not judge God's ways whilst they are in progress. Wait till the plan is complete. Wait till the tapestry is finished and you can see the other side, where the pattern will be worked out. Wait till the silver paper is torn off the worsted work and the blending of the colors is disclosed. Wait till you have got out of the vale to the mountain brow. Wait till in the light of eternity God can call you aside and reveal to you his purposes. Meanwhile trust. All his ways are pleasantness and his paths peace."

Once again we say : —

The fact that you are in the world proves that you are indispensable to God, and the fact that you are where you are, if it has not been of your own choosing, proves that God needs you there to work out his plan.

You see only the " wrong side " of your life, like the weaver of tapestry. God sees the " right side," and weaves on, and shall until the work is ended.

> " My life is but the weaving
>   Between my God and me ;
> I may but choose the colors
>   He weaveth steadily.
> Full oft he weaveth sorrow,
>   And I in foolish pride
> Forget he sees the upper,
>   And I the under, side."

SUGGESTIONS FOR TO-DAY

1. Trust for to-day, where you cannot understand him.

2. Remember he said, "What I do thou knowest not *now*, but thou shalt know hereafter." Wait for the nereafter.

3. Tell him over and over, as the way seems closing up before you, that you will never doubt him.

Eighteenth Day

"For his name's sake."

THERE could no greater blessing come into your life than that you should look up in every trying circumstance, and say, —

> "Lead thou me on
> O'er moor and fen, o'er crag and torrent, till
> The night is gone."

But we do not need to plead for this leadership. He is pledged to it by the greatness of his own great name. The name indicates the honor and character of God, and these are committed to your care and mine. "The leading of a saint is guaranteed by their immutability." His name is —

Wonderful. You can think of nothing in the way of blessing he will not press into your life.

Counsellor. You can imagine no circumstance

so trying that his judgment will fail you, nothing so trivial that he will turn away from the settlement of it.

The Everlasting Father. The love of a father, the patience of a father, the helpfulness of a father, are his; but they are to be multiplied by infinity, and they are yours forever. Claim their helpfulness in your life, they are your inheritance.

The Prince of peace. By that name he is pledged to you to bring rest in place of restlessness, harmony instead of confusion, and peace in the place of strife and worry.

"Peace, perfect peace, in this dark world of sin ·
The blood of Jesus whispers peace within.

"Peace, perfect peace, by thronging duties pressed:
To do the will of Jesus, — this is rest.

"It is enough: earth's struggles soon shall cease,
And Jesus call us to heaven's perfect peace."

SUGGESTIONS FOR TO-DAY

Remember three things give us the right to use a name: —

1. A legal relation. You have a right to use the name of your partner in business, and you are bound to him by a law which cannot be broken.

2. A life relation. You have the right to use the name of your father, and you are born from above, having the very life of God.

3. A love relation. Your wife has the right and the privilege of your name, and you are bound to God by a love which nothing in time or eternity can affect.

Because of these things you have the right to claim the blessing of his name, for the sake of it he is pledged to hear your claim and honor it.

Nineteenth Day

" Yea, though I WALK through the valley."

THERE is probably no verse in Scripture with which we are more familiar than this. When the fear of death has taken hold upon us, we have said these words; and, when death was actually upon our loved ones, with shining faces they whispered this text.

There are two interpretations for this expression, the first of which is that the reference is not so much to the future as to the present. " A valley is a low place with mountains on either side. Enemies may be posted on these mountains to shoot their arrows at the traveller, as ever was the case in the East. The Psalmist, however, said he would fear no evil, not even the fiery darts of the wicked one; for the Lord was with him."

And David meant to say that in every trial of life, when enemies were on every hand, we need not lose hope. All the promises of God are ours for such a time as that, and the music of heaven cheers us on our way.

One of my friends, the Rev. Ford C. Ottman, has said : —

"One night from the old ruined castle of the Drachenfels I saw the sun set over the western hills, and heard the chiming of the evening bells along the Rhine ; but darkness began to gather, and I must make my way to the little town at the foot of the mountain.

"Perhaps I was half-way down, when I came upon one of the most beautiful spots that it has been my privilege ever to see ; it was a veritable bower of fairies ; the branches of the trees were twined together ; the moss was softer than the softest carpet under your feet.

"Passing through, while the shadows of the evening fell, that place suddenly became vocal with song.   Never have I heard such music as that.   I stood still in perfect wonder. It seemed almost like coming to the gates of heaven.

"When I arrived at the foot of the mountain, I told a friend of this experience. 'O,' said he, 'you were in the Nachtigallenthal, the Vale of the Nightingales ; they sing there every night.'"

When the sun of your life has seemed to set

and hope is well-nigh dead, and no star of promised day seems to rise in the sky of your life, listen. You will hear him say, "I will never leave thee"; and your soul will make a quick response, "I will fear no evil."

There will be discouragements to-day and every day; but, as there is no valley without a well in it or a spring of water, you may in the midst of it all stoop and drink of the delight of his presence with you. Did he not say, I am with you in all your ways?

"IT IS BETTER FURTHER ON"

I hear it singing, singing sweetly,
    Softly in an undertone;
Singing as if God had taught it,
    "It is better further on."

Night and day it sings the same song,
    Sings it while I sit alone.
Sings it so the heart can hear it,
    "It is better further on."

Sits upon the grave and sings it,
    Sings it when the heart would groan,
Sings it when the shadows darken,
    "It is better further on."

Further on ! how much further ?
    Count the milestones one by one ?
No, no counting, only trusting,
    " It is better further on."

SUGGESTIONS FOR TO-DAY

1. What if the clouds are above you ? Remember that ever since that day when " a cloud received him out of their sight " he has been behind every cloud. James Whitcomb Riley's verse is full of truth, —

" But always keep rememberin', when cares your path
    enshroud,
That God has lots of sunshine to spill behind the cloud."

2. Remember that it is a " walk through," and you need not stop to-day where you halted yesterday.

3. What if you did fail ? His love has not in any way wavered toward you. Those were sweet words of Browning's : —

" Have you found your life distasteful ?
    My life did, and does, smell sweet.
Was your youth of pleasure wasteful ?
    Mine I saved, and hold complete.

" Do your joys with age diminish ?
    When mine fail me, I 'll complain.

Must in death your daylight finish?
  My sun sets to rise again.

" I find earth not gray, but rosy ;
  Heaven not grim, but fair of hue.
Do I stoop? I pluck a posy ;
  Do I stand and stare? All 's blue."

Twentieth Day

"I walk through the valley of the shadow of death."

But there is another application, and it is the one most precious to us, possibly because most often given. The words speak of that time when we may pass by the way of death into His presence whom having not seen we have loved.

"'I walk,' says the Psalmist; and dead sheep cannot walk, they must be carried."

"As if the believer did not quicken his pace when he came to die, but calmly walked with God. To walk indicates the steady advance of a soul, which knows its road, knows its end, resolves to follow the path, feels quite safe, and is therefore perfectly calm and composed. The dying saint is not in a flurry; he does not run as if he were alarmed, nor stand still as though he would go no further. He is not confounded nor ashamed, and therefore keeps to his old pace."

Observe also that he is walking *through* the valley.

"We go through the dark tunnel of death and emerge into the light of immortality. We do not die; we do but sleep to wake in glory. Death is not the house, but the porch; not the goal, but the passage to it."

It is well called a valley. "The storm breaks on the mountain; but the valley is the place of quietude, and thus full often the last days of the Christian are the most peaceful in his whole career. The mountain is bleak and bare, but the valley is rich with golden sheaves, and many a saint has reaped more joy and knowledge when he came to die than he ever knew while he lived." These are the words of the sainted Spurgeon. I doubt not that if he could speak to-day he would only add to the beauty of his description of our going home to be with Christ.

"Lie still in the darkness;
    Sleep safe in the night,
The Lord is a watchman,
    The Lamb is a light.
Jehovah, he holdeth
    The sea and the land,

The earth in the hollow
Of his mighty hand.
All 's well in the darkness,
All 's well in the light,
The Lamb is a watchman,
The Lamb is a light.''

SUGGESTIONS FOR TO-DAY

1. This may be your last day upon earth. If so, would your pace through the valley be the same as your walk of yesterday?

2. If "to live is Christ and to die is gain," and your life is anything less than Christ, then what will your death be?

3. If the path of the just is as the shining light that shineth more and more unto the perfect day, then what is it that casts the shadows on your path? It must be something between you and the light.

4. If to-morrow should mark your entrance into glory, then live to-day as you will wish you had when you see him.

Twenty-first Day

"I will fear no evil."

HE does not say, "There shall not be any evil," but, "I shall not *fear* it."

It must have been because he knew that he had only to do with the shadow of death, for death in its substance had been removed and only its shadow remained.

"Some one has said that where there is a shadow there must be a light somewhere, and so there is. Death stands by the side of the highway in which we have to travel, and the light of heaven shining upon him throws a shadow across our path. Let us then rejoice that there is a light beyond. Nobody is afraid of a shadow, for a shadow cannot stop a man's pathway even for a moment. The shadow of a dog cannot bite; the shadow of a sword cannot kill; the shadow of death cannot destroy us." Why therefore should we be afraid?

"There is no fear in love. Perfect love casteth out fear. Nothing else can do it. You may argue against fear. You may deride it. You may try and shame it. But all will be in vain. If you would master it, you must expel it by the trust which is born of love. A man comes home fain, and famished. His nature craves for food; but as he enters into his house, he learns that his child suddenly stricken with fever is lying at the point of death, and in a moment he has forgotten his hunger in the paroxysm of love and grief with which he bends over the tiny feverish form, and hastens to moisten the dry lips. Thus the lower passions are subdued in the soul by the higher, and so it happens that the most timid spirit which is conscious of the presence of the good Shepherd can sing as it passes onward through the gloom, and its notes vibrate with the buoyancy of a courage which cannot flinch or falter."

SUGGESTIONS FOR TO-DAY

1. If you are living where God intended you should, if this valley of shadows be accepted as a present-day experience, then Christ will be between you and every ill.

2. It is not God's plan that anything should separate you from him; and, if anything stands

between you, it is either with your permission or by your choice.

3. Evil cannot separate you from him at any time. The table on which was placed the show-bread of the tabernacle had about the bread a golden band, and a hand's breadth away was a second band; so that, if any pieces fell away, it must be over these two golden bands, which was impossible. Round about us are the two strong arms of God; and, whether the psalm be present or future, I can say, " I will fear no evil."

Twenty-second Day

"Thou art with me."

Do you notice the change in the person of the pronoun here? In other instances the Psalmist has spoken of his Lord in the third person; but now, as he comes into the shadows, he comes nearer to him, and says "*Thou*."

It is all very well to speak in general terms when all goes well with us; but the darkness is upon us and the heart-strings almost snap; it is better far to avail ourselves of our birthright privilege and say, "*Thou* art with me;" I will fear no evil.

Doubtless this day shall mean something of disappointment and trial, but the sting will be taken out of it when we remember that *He is* with us "whose fan is in his hand." The fan was a rude instrument used to separate the chaff from the wheat, and our Lord is dealing with us for the same reason. He will not permit more of trial than we can stand or need.   Let us rejoice that the fan is not in the hands of our enemies — they would make us suffer too much, nor in the hands of our friends — for they would make it too easy, but in *His* who walks with us every hour of every day.

SUGGESTIONS FOR TO-DAY

1. Remember that whom the Lord loveth he chastiseth.

2. Picture Job's suffering and Paul's trials; then thank God that, while you have nothing so heavy, you do have Christ.

3. Remember that if we suffer with him, we shall also share in his glory.   Then thank God for trial.

Twenty-third Day

"Thy rod."

A SHEPHERD'S rod is that with which he defends his sheep. It was not unlikely that in passing through the valley serious danger would meet the flock, and the shepherd's business is to drive the evil away. Surely this is a comfort for us.

There will be danger before you to-day. Temptations will spring upon you from most unexpected places. You will fail but for the Shepherd's care.

There are certain things which may surely be likened to the shepherd's rod.

1. The Bible. When our Lord met the devil in the time of his temptation, to all of his insidious suggestions he said, "It is written." This is the real secret of victory.

You cannot drive him away with holy feelings, with heavenly experiences, but only with God's word well known, and well used.

2. Prayer. There are so many forms of prayer, none of which are more helpful than the ejaculatory. If we pray only at stated times, Satan may be there ready to tempt us. But the prayer that rises in the midst of business and when you are suddenly beset by danger takes him unawares and makes him flee from us. Prayer is like the shepherd's rod.

SUGGESTIONS FOR TO-DAY

1. Learn at least one new verse of Scripture for each day. Wield it as the sword of the Spirit.

2. Read one chapter of the book of Proverbs daily. Singularly enough, there are just thirty-one. Then live in the atmosphere of the portion you read.

3. Pray often. "Be instant in prayer." Let prayer strike the *key-note* for the day, and prayer through the day keep you in harmony with the key-note; and the day will be a song of victory.

Twenty-fourth Day

"And thy staff."

THE shepherd's staff is his crook, bent or hooked at one end. No shepherd is complete without it. It is used for three different purposes. Beneath it the sheep pass to be counted as they go into the fold. By means of it the sheep fallen into the pit are rescued. In the hands of the shepherd it is sometimes used for correction or punishment.

Let it encourage you this day to know that your name is not unknown to the Lord. In the Old Testament days the high priest wore over his heart the breastplate on which were inscribed the names of the children of Israel. Our names in these New Testament days are written over his heart. God sees us there.

But, alas! in spite of all this, many of us have fallen. David did. Peter did. But He whose name is love stoops to lift us up. You cannot get away from his love. David came up from the pit to write his best psalms, and Peter to preach one of the world's greatest sermons. So may you.

Many of us have needed the rod of correction. If your heart is aching and your home desolate, it would be well to stop and ask whether this is not God speaking to you in this way because you would not hear in any other.

SUGGESTIONS FOR TO-DAY

1. Remember that temptation is a compliment paid you by the tempter. He sees that there is something in you worth the having, and tempts you that he may gain it.

2. Sin is yielding; it is opening the door, permitting the sinful thought for which you were in no way responsible to tarry with you.

3. Remember that God will take your part against sin if you will let him.

Twenty-fifth Day

"Thou preparest a table before me."

THERE is a sudden change here in the figure of the psalm. In many of the preceding thoughts we have been walking, but now the picture is that of feasting.

But this is always true; when one walks with God, he always feasts.

And it is a prepared feast; God had our needs in mind when he spread it. There is there that which will overcome our discontent, and there is food which will cause us all to rejoice even in the face of disappointment.

"I say it over and over, and yet again to-day
　It rests my heart as surely as it did yesterday;
　　'It is the Lord's appointment;'
　　Whatever my work may be,
　　I am sure in my heart of hearts
　　He has offered it for me.

" I must say it over and over, and yet again to-day,
  For my work is somewhat different from yesterday ;
     ' It is the Lord's appointment ; '
     It quiets my restless will
     Like voice of tender mother,
     And my heart and will are still.

" I will say it over and over, this and every day,
  Whatsoever the Master orders, come what may,
     ' It is the Lord's appointment ; '
     For only his love can see
     What is wisest, best, and right,
     What is truly good for me."

He places before us just that which may pro-
duce well-rounded, symmetrical Christian character.   But, as we might starve in the presence of
a well-laden board, so in spite of all God's
gracious provision we may remain children in
weakness, and miserably fail ; on the other hand,
he that eateth shall never hunger.

SUGGESTIONS FOR TO-DAY

1. Whatever other interpretation may be given
to our feeding upon Christ, this at least is true : we
must take time to do it, and time must be taken
to-day to satisfy the soul's needs.

2. It is not what we eat, but what is digested

that gives strength to the body; so it is what you shall meditate upon to-day that will make you strong in the Lord.

3. Gratitude is the golden key that unlocks and keeps open the rich storehouse of God's best gifts; so make your requests known " with thanksgiving " for the prepared table.

4. " Be careful for nothing, prayerful for everything, thankful for anything."   Phil. 4 : 6.

Twenty-sixth Day

" In the presence of mine enemies."

" THE good man has his enemies; he would not be like his Lord if he had not. If we were without enemies, we might fear that we were not the friends of God, for the friendship of the world is enmity with God. Yet see the quietude of the godly man in spite of and in the face of his enemies."

There was an old Roman custom, which may have prevailed even in David's time, which would shed light on this part of the psalm. When a soldier had won a victory and taken the enemy prisoners, a feast was made for him, and the captives were bound to the pillars of the banqueting-hall; and in their presence he was made to sit down and eat. This certainly may be realized in your experience and mine.

A man's foes are they of his own household, and our worst enemies are from within. With some it is temper; with others, pride; with still others, unholy thoughts; and with many, the disposition to actual outbreaking sin. But there is deliverance from all, and there may be so complete a submission to Christ that he, becoming the master of your life, will bind them all and cause you to feast in their presence.

SUGGESTIONS FOR TO-DAY

1. Open your eyes to the fact that you are not free from danger. Sin is not dead, and the old nature may be easily revived.

2. Remember that sin is mightier than your resolution or your will. Determination not to sin is not the secret of victory.

3. Put your whole life in the undisputed control of Christ. He is the secret of victory always and everywhere.

Twenty-seventh Day

"Thou anointest my head with oil."

"Why anoint the head with oil? Ah! David has in mind a picture of the high priest in the sanctuary. In the most holy place of the tabernacle God revealed himself, but a curtain hung before it, and no one could pass that curtain and look upon God and live; but once a year, on the great day of atonement, it was the privilege of the high priest to pass within the veil, and stand in the presence of God. Just before the veil opened, and he passed in, his head must be anointed with oil. Oil is the symbol of the Holy Spirit. This anointing was the symbol of the Spirit's work preparing him to go in before God. It is written, 'Without holiness, no man shall see the Lord.' We are not yet ready to come face to face with God, but when the good Shepherd is leading us through the valley, and we come to heaven's gate, just before we pass in, the Holy Spirit will finish his work of sanctification, and we, by him, will be prepared to meet God. 'Thou anointest my head with oil.'"

Yet there is an anointing for the present time, which each may claim.

1. Oil to make the face shine. Ps. 104 : 15. It is not possible to come in touch with the Holy Ghost, and not reveal the fact in our lives.

2. The oil of gladness. Ps. 45 : 7. Satan cannot rob us of our life, but he may deprive us of our joy. It is the work of Christ to bring us to heaven, but it is the work of the Spirit to bring heaven to us now.

SUGGESTIONS FOR TO-DAY

1. Whatever your past experience may have been in Christ, claim a fresh anointing for to-day from the Holy Ghost.

2. Remember that every Christian is a priest, but he cannot execute the priestly office without unction, and hence we must go day by day to God the Holy Ghost, that we may have our heads anointed with oil.

3. Remember that a priest in touch with any dead thing could not execute his office. Ask yourself over and over to-day, " Is my heart right in the sight of God ? "

4. Live for one day, at least, a separated life.

Twenty-eighth Day

"My cup runneth over."

"He had not only a fulness of abundance, but of redundance. Those that have this happiness must carry their cup upright, and see that it overflow into their poor brethren's emptier vessels."

"The showers that fall upon the highest mountains should glide into the lowest valleys."

The fact that you are a Christian may without doubt assure you a safe entrance into heaven, but it may not mean that you are much of a blessing to your friends about you. God makes the life to overflow, that other men's lives may be touched with your power. For it is only the *overflow* of your life that proves a blessing to your friends and kindred.

It is the overflow of the Nile that makes the valley of the Nile fruitful.

SUGGESTIONS FOR TO-DAY

1. Remember that it is one thing to have life, but quite another to have the life more abundant : which have you ?

2. God has certainly promised you that you may have both. See John 10 : 10. Claim that promise now.

3. If there is no overflow, it must be because some obstacle is between you and him. Ask him to search you and make the work complete.

4. Trust him to fill you and to keep you filled.

Twenty-ninth Day

"Goodness and mercy shall follow me."

"This sentence may be read, ' Only goodness and mercy shall follow me,' for there shall be unmingled mercy in our history. These twin guardian angels will always be at my back and my beck. Just as when great princes go abroad they must not go unattended, so it is with the believer. Goodness and mercy follow him always. 'All the days of his life,' the black days as well as the bright days, the days of fasting as well as the days of feasting, the dreary days of winter as well as the bright days of summer. Goodness supplies our needs, and mercy blots out our sins."

It is Mr. Meyer who says that. The shepherd always goes before his sheep; goodness and mercy like shepherd dogs come after. What a protection for the sheep! how safe the journey may be!

HE LEADETH ME

" In pastures green ?   Not always : sometimes He
Who knoweth best, in kindness leadeth me
In weary ways, where heavy shadows be ;

" Out of the sunshine, warm and soft and bright,
Out of the sunshine into the darkest night.
I oft would faint with sorrow and affright,

" Only for this : I know He holds my hand ;
So, whether in green or desert land,
I trust, although I may not understand.

" And by still waters ?   No, not always so ;
Ofttimes the heavy tempests round me blow,
And o'er my soul the waves and billows go ;

" But, when the storm beats loudest, and I cry
Aloud for help, the Master standeth by,
And whispers to my soul, ' Lo, it is I ! '

" Above the tempest would I hear him say,
' Beyond this darkness lies the perfect day,
In every path of thine I lead the way.'

" So, whether on the hill-tops high and fair
I dwell, or in sunless valleys where
The shadows lie, what matter ?   He is there.

"And more than this : where'er the pathways lead,
He gives no helpless, broken reed,
But his own hand, sufficient for my need

"So, where He leads me I can safely go,
And in the blest hereafter I shall know
Why, in his wisdom, he hath led me so."

SUGGESTIONS FOR TO-DAY

1. Remember this is one of "all the days," and God had you in mind when he made the pledge of help.

2. Be sure the God who kept his word with Abraham, Isaac, and Jacob will not begin to break his word with you.

3. Trust him when you cannot understand him; rejoice even when darkness seems to settle about you.

4. Walk boldly, knowing he is leading, and goodness and mercy are following close behind.

Thirtieth Day

"I will dwell in the house of the Lord forever."

A servant abideth not in the house forever; but the son doth. And we are the children of God.

"While I am here, I will be a child at home with my God. The whole world shall be his house to me; and, when I ascend into the upper chamber, I shall not change my company, nor even change the house. I shall only be in the upper story forever." — *Spurgeon*.

"This should be at once the crown of all our hopes for the future and the one great lesson taught us by all the vicissitudes of life."

There is an end in which it shall be made plain why we had darkness here and sorrowed many times, and as we look back over all the way, we shall find that every road, crooked though it seemed, led heavenward.

"The light of the Word shines brighter and brighter
   As wider and wider God opens my eyes;
   My trials and burdens seem lighter and lighter,
   And fairer and fairer the heavenly prize.

"The wealth of this world seems poorer and poorer
   As further and further it fades from my sight;
   The prize of my calling seems surer and surer,
   As straighter and straighter I walk in the light.

"My waiting on Jesus seems dearer and dearer
   As longer and longer I lean on his breast;
   Without him, I'm nothing, seems clearer and clearer,
   And more and more sweetly in Jesus I rest.

"My joy in my Saviour is growing and growing,
   And stronger and stronger I trust in his word;
   My peace like a river is flowing and flowing,
   As harder and harder I lean on the Lord."

SUGGESTIONS FOR TO-DAY

1. Do not complain at the trials and vexations of this short journey. This is not your home, and these are only incidents by the way.

2. Ask God for this day to help you live as Jesus would if he were in your place.

3. Remember that temptation, trial, sorrow, and disappointment all help in the weaving of the robe which we shall wear up yonder.

Thirty-first Day

Conclusion.

In the war of the Rebellion a little drummer boy was injured in the battle. He was carried into the hospital, and one of the soldiers near by heard the doctors say the case was fatal. Immediately he said, "Doctor, if this is true, I must send word to his mother, for I promised to look after this boy."

The letter went away to the North, and as soon as possible the mother came. The doctors met her at the hospital to say that she could not see her boy. He had fallen into a stupor, and if aroused would die in a paroxysm of pain; for he was then beyond all hope.

But you cannot bind up a mother's love with physician's rules, and so she said, "Doctor, if you will permit me to go in, I will not speak to him; but I should like to sit beside him as he dies." Permission was given her, and she took her place by his side. She kept her word and said nothing to her child; but, when she saw by the expression of his face that he was suffering, she leaned over and put her hand upon his brow.

There is something peculiar about the touch of a mother's hand, and the dying soldier boy felt it. His eyes did not open, but she saw his lips moving; and, bending over, she heard him saying over and over, "I knew you 'd come; I knew you 'd come." And this I say of our good Shepherd. O thou Shepherd of the sheep, in every hour of trial and time of disappointment and night of misunderstanding "I know that thou wilt come."

And he will.

SUGGESTIONS FOR TO—DAY

Say over and over the whole psalm, emphasizing the personal and possessive pronouns as here given : —

PSALM 23

David's confidence in God

A Psalm of David

The LORD is *my* shepherd; *I* shall not want.
2. He maketh *me* to lie down in green pastures .
he leadeth *me* beside the still waters.

3. He restoreth *my* soul: he leadeth *me* in the paths of righteousness for his name's sake.

4. Yea, though *I* walk through the valley of the shadow of death, *I* will fear no evil: for thou art with *me*; thy rod and thy staff they comfort *me*.

5. Thou preparest a table before *me* in the presence of *mine* enemies: thou anointest *my* head with oil; *my* cup runneth over.

6. Surely goodness and mercy shall follow *me* all the days of *my* life; and *I* will dwell in the house of the LORD forever.

THE END